Praise for coming to awareness



Haikus are like meditation bell 'Ding!'s, sudden bursts of clarity illuminating the moment. This wonderful book is one 'Ding!' after another.
"I apologize / to my mouth for all the meals / I let it sleep through." 'Ding!'
You could think of these haikus as seeds of contemplation, or as flashing reminders, "Wake Up! Wake Up! Wake Up!"
Or both. A perfect gift for a meditating friend. Or yourself.

Sylvia Boorstein, author of *Happiness Is an Inside Job*

David Daniel shares the wisdom he has encountered in meditation retreats with us all in these peaceful but striking haikus that awaken our minds and charge our hungry hearts to joy and to peace. They bear witness to the power of silence and mind-emptying to bring us all home again for the work for compassion that follows from a quiet heart. Read these haikus and Be Awakened! Thank you, David Daniel!

Rev. Dr. Matthew Fox, author of *A Way to God*

I have found that to express that which is inexpressible, one must enter the realm of poetry. Sometime the more words you use to describe the ineffable, the murkier and more misleading it gets. These haikus are the perfect expressions of a journey that sparkles and invites us fully into the next step. They are succinct, concise, profound, delightful and intriguing. Here is a book that inspires me to enter the mystery while lightening the burdens of my heart.

Rabbi Shefa Gold, author of *Are We There Yet? Travel as a Spiritual Path*

Utilizing the deceptively simple structure of Japanese haiku poetry, David Daniel Klipper offers us a feast of wise, funny, deep, sweet, poignant and utterly compelling gems of personal spiritual wisdom. On the surface, an "easy read," but don't skim! These treats are too rich. Allow each one to be a mind-heart mediation, and savor where this takes you.

Rabbi Marcia Prager, author of *The Path of Blessing, Experiencing the Energy and Abundance of the Divine*

With surprising grace, Klipper captures moments that transcend the ordinary and point toward a shared universal. Read these gently. Chew on the sounds. Return to find what you have not found before. Here is a treasury of possibilities.

Rabbi Ted Falcon, PhD, co-author of *Finding Peace Through Spiritual Practice*.

"The People of the Book are about to become the People of the Haiku. With a keen eye for paradox and a transcendent wit, David Daniel Klipper synthesizes sanctity with succinctness to bring us a soaring exercise in mindfulness. His "haiku from silent meditation retreats" just might find their way as a companion to the siddur on every synagogue shelf."

Rabbi Joshua Hammerman, author of *Mensch-Marks: Life-Lessons of a Human Rabbi*

In this collection of haikus, David Daniel Klipper has captured a great deal of the wisdom and open-hearted connection that comes in a week of silent meditation. His haikus illuminate the precious insights of practice in small yet deep bites. Reading this book, you might want to come on a retreat yourself and if you have already been on one, you'll recognize your memoirs.

Rabbi Jeff Roth, author of *Jewish Meditation Practices for Everyday Life: Awakening Your Heart, Connecting with God*

Encountering the Divine is an individual experience. How one gets there and what one finds there is unique to the seeker. As unique as the encounter itself is the process by which it is shared with others. History is replete with mystics who express their wonder and awe through song, poetry and prose, through art in all its forms. David Daniel Klipper's beautiful expression of the inner life in silence comes through his poetic lens and inspires further contemplation in the reader, even as it entertains and invites a chuckle. His work is unique and wonderful!

Rabbi Nadya Gross, co-author of *Embracing Wisdom, Soaring in the Second Half of Life*

It is with joy and gratitude that I let you know the sweetness of sitting with your gift of haikus. Each one is a blessing, delicious in all it offers, yet the flow of one to another is an arc that is playful and profound, real and true and pure. I so appreciate you sharing this precious unfolding with me. I will return to these many times.

Tovah Zeh, spiritual teacher

# coming to awareness

## haiku from silent meditation retreats

David Daniel Klipper

To Ya'el,

with appreciation for the work you are doing and the contribution you are making.

blessings,

David Daniel

ISBN-13: 9798584942724

Cover design by Denise Barringer
Printed in the United States of America

opening to God

in seventeen syllables?

are you kidding me?

*this is for my wife*
*who is my partner in life*
*the home for my soul*

*for Ted, my teacher*
*and my friend, with thanks, love and*
*appreciation*

Introduction

As a sometime poet and writer since my teens, I have always appreciated and enjoyed the haiku form. Often it seems that these little three-line poems, with their 5-7-5 syllable arrangement, can convey more meaning and heart than poems many times their length.

I have also admired the directness and presence of mystical poets such as Hafiz, Rumi, Kabir, Meister Eckhart, and others. The level of wisdom and consciousness they had attained, combined with the nature of the subject about which they wrote, enabled them to speak very directly toward the reader. I have found that the haiku form, particularly haiku that address issues of spirituality, similarly allows for this type of direct address and intimacy with the reader, while at the same time leaving an open space for the reader to discover his/her own meanings in the poem.

A number of months ago I wrote a haiku about prayer for my spiritual director. It read:

prayer is a lie
that I have to believe in
with all of my heart.

I found that this haiku well captured the complications and paradoxes that were in my thoughts, feelings and practices about prayer. It spoke very directly to people who confront some of these same issues and struggles with prayer, while being opaque or confusing to others. But for those who understood, a wealth of meaning was conveyed.

I continued to write spiritual haiku from time to time as they emerged. Then, in August 2016 I attended a silent seven-day

Jewish meditation retreat. By the second day I experienced what turned out to be an explosion of creativity. Although we were not allowed to write during the meditation periods (and in fact were not supposed to write at all), I composed 52 haiku in these seven days. I found part of my meditation practice consisted of trying to remember the theme and the last line of a haiku (and sometimes two or three of them) until the next break when I could write them down. This was perhaps not exactly the one-pointed attention the meditation teachers had in mind. ☺

Part of my urgency in wanting to record these haiku was that I realized that I had entered a realm of consciousness (for substantial periods of time) that was very different from my day-to-day consciousness. I knew that it might be difficult for me to recall or describe what it was like to be in this expanded state of consciousness.

There is a sentence that occurs at the end of paragraphs in a number of mystical Hasidic writings. The words *hameivin yavin* essentially mean "those who understand will understand." While I had always found the tautological nature of this sentence to be intensely irritating, during the retreat I understood its basic truth—that there are some insights that can be grasped only if the individual has had the experiences required to develop the necessary perspective.

So, what led me to record these haiku was my fear that when I returned to the work-a-day world and couldn't be in silence from wake up to sleep time, I would also lose access to the states of consciousness I was experiencing.

I went to the retreat again a year later and had the same experience of expanded consciousness and creativity expressing itself in haiku. These succinct poems helped me clarify what I was thinking and feeling. However, I think their true purpose is to wake me up, even if only for an instant. I hope that they

do the same for you as another sojourner on the journey.
*hameivin yavin*

A word about words, especially a particular word that provokes many reactions: God. As you can tell from the haiku above, I have a somewhat unconventional (and paradoxical) conception of God. Please substitute whatever word(s) or concept(s) work for you. I am not endorsing any particular belief system, including my own (my belief system believes all belief systems take us away from our experience and we spend too much time justifying them).

So please, go ahead and join me in the experience of the silent retreat. Come more than once. I hope that it takes you to places of deep holiness and gives you a sense of the richness of experience that awaits us at all times if we are able to open to it.

Don't forget to enjoy the moment!

much more important<br>than the destination is<br>our journey – blessings

## *Theology*

prayer is a lie
that I have to believe in
with all of my heart

my mind tells me that
prayer is a lie. God thinks
that's pretty funny

the deepest teachings
before you're broken open
sound like blasphemy

take one step forward
but then you fall two steps back.
still, three steps toward God.

it's terrifying
knowing we don't know God's will
what about my plans?

in the now, there's no
spiritual path, just a
spiritual dot

living completely
in the now there is no hope
instead there is joy

it was raining, so
I wrote a want ad for God
She applied at once!

while I'm watching it,
is the sunrise less lonely?
I certainly am

I now realize
God does not care about me
yet I am so loved

living in the now
would I be aware of it
if I died tonight?

## *Struggle*

I'm bored, fidgety
my mind flits, darts, jumps around
where is the silence?

my mind is racing
racing, racing, racing. what
am I running from?

booze, drugs, sex, sugar
desperate to fill up my
lonely addict heart

I knew that I was
a creature of appetites
but to this extent?

now I count my breaths
now I'm getting distracted
now I count my breaths

meditate three hours
for what? thirty seconds
of being awake

I sit on my bench
inhale, then exhale. repeat
and I stay asleep

I sit on my bench
inhale, then exhale. repeat
and I am awake

I need to hurry
so I can go and be still.  what's
wrong with this picture?

God, where have you gone?
my eyes are closed, my ears plugged
God, where have I gone?

a thought!  my mind wants
to leap on it, instead of
staying in the now

## *Progress*

I've achieved success
on the meditation bench
my big toes hurt less!

here's my day.  sit.  walk.
sit.  walk.  sit.  eat.  sit some more.
so what's the big rush?

THESE AREN'T JUST PRAYERS!
sing them with full intention
you might awaken

5:30 am
time to wake up and go sit
it's still dark outside

I need the music
it lifts me above the words
to air and sunlight

I feel scared and shamed
there is nothing more to do
but forgive myself.

how to heal my pain?
love the quiet, sad, scared child
he suffers so much

this wound in my heart –
may I come to embrace it
as a true blessing

it's a hard teaching –
finding God inside the pain
the fear and the shame

# *Food*

learning to eat slow
eighty minutes just for lunch
the taste is amazing

a new discovery
chewing should always be done
slowly, with eyes closed.

mindlessly reading
trapped turning page after page
what a waste of taste!

You are so great, God
thanks for creating the taste
of a banana

put food in my mouth
it chews madly, terrified
I won't get enough

it is so quiet
I'm chewing my banana
it's all I can hear

I apologize
to my mouth for all the meals
I let it sleep through

the melon explodes,
overwhelming my taste buds
incomparable!

# *Insight*

The doorway to God
has but a single handle
it is on my side.

anyone who claims
never to think of sex while
sitting, is lying

I stumble blindly
searching for the love that is
already within

I crave importance
it's never enough.  I'm sad
for that lonely self

I am the ocean,
thinking I'm a wave, and that
I'll die on the beach

you may want to climb
the holy mountain, but you
must trudge through the swamp.

my great delusion
I need to control the world
what a waste of time.

fix mind on one point
my ego’s afraid it's a
kind of death.  it is

I just learned something
I can really use.  slow my
breathing, slow my mind

the more desperate
I am for God, the closer
God is in the need.

it's not really hard
finding the God within.  I
just need to unfold.

# *Joy of Silence*

I sit.  I barely breathe
in the center of the world
slow silence awaits

God's prompt is my breath
each inhale is nectar.  who
could want more than this?

I thought my insides
were empty, full of pain. who
knew there was such light?

being present to
this breath. so much better than
medals or parades

what's unbearable
at speed becomes nurturing
in gentle slowness.

the door to myself
is open. I'm amazed its
so spacious inside.

a sphere of silence
revolves and shines waves of bliss
from my singing heart.

no expectations,
let life come just as it comes,
no disappointments.

I thought that Presence
was passive. No! It is a
powerful embrace!

God is patiently
waiting behind the next breath
for you to stop by

my life in six words:
this breath, I can be joyous
that's all that I need

sitting in stillness
I know I'm a container
for absolute love

the words of the chant
swirling amidst my silence
hold me tenderly

every instant
I see there is so much joy
nobody told me

the nectar of the
universe. overflowing
with pure compassion

I can no longer
sing the words of the prayer
I forget to breathe.

I thought there were words
this is a place of no words
the heart of silence

it is refreshing
my breath breathes me, pure, and I
breathe along, grateful

the quiet after
a prayer is sung shimmers
in the deep silence.

I sit and breathe in
the ordinary silence
moment by moment

I'm grateful knowing
I need not fear the silence…
where You await me.

I feel the stillness.
All I can say to God is
"Take me! Please take me!"

as my soul unfolds
I embrace the rising light
how can I not love?

silence holds all sounds,
speaks all words, lifts all voices,
contains all wisdom

# *Farewell*

please let my life change
let this be more than just a
week without talking

I was scared coming
now I'm scared to be going
I live between fears

will I remember
how much I need to stay slow?
from stillness comes joy

how will I know that
I'm going too fast when I'm too
speedy to notice?

if I get to leave
something behind, let it be
negative self-talk

# *Epilogue*

Holy Blessed One,
unfold me into brightness
fill my soul with joy!

# *Acknowledgements*

It may not take a village to make a book, but it certainly takes a village to make an author. Gratitude to Rabbis Jeff Roth and Joanna Katz, Sylvia Boorstein and Norman Fischer for their teaching in the silent meditation retreats that were the direct impetus for this book; Rabbis Shefa Gold, Nadya Gross, Josh Hammerman, Marcia Prager, Rev. Matthew Fox, Sylvia Boorstein and Tovah Zeh for writing such lovely blurbs; Hazzan Diana Brewer and Rabbi Caryn Aviv for their encouragement and delight in my haiku; Karen Olio for her years of love and support; Angela Howes for her editing; Denise Barringer for her cover design; all of my teachers and spiritual directors for the learning and training I've received; all of my students, supervisees and spiritual directees for the amazing amount they've taught me and how they've made me a better person; Rabbi Ted Falcon for his teaching and unconditional love; and most of all, my wife Barbara for her steadfast love and support for over 40 years. I could not do this without her.

# About the author:

David Daniel Klipper is an ordained Rabbinic Pastor. He feels blessed to be able to serve as a spiritual director, supervisor of spiritual directors and CPE (Clinical Pastoral Education) Educator. He and his wife Barbara live in Cape Cod, MA and Sarasota, FL.

For more information and his blog, please go to:
www.daviddanielklipper.com

Made in the USA
Middletown, DE
02 November 2021